GIVE THE GIFT!

10 Fulfilling Ways to Raise a Lifetime Reader

by Matthew Gollub

illustrated by Larry Nolte

TORTUGA PRESS Santa Rosa, California

With thanks

To my mother Lorraine Gollub who read to me when I was small,
To parents, grandparents, and caregivers everywhere
who somehow give the gift every day, and
To the countless educators who contributed insights—
You are my inspiration.
— M.G.

To Graham, champion reader.
— L.N.

Other popular books written or published by Matthew Gollub

Books in English with audio CD:
• *The Jazz Fly* • *Gobble, Quack, Moon*
• *Wooleycat's Musical Theater* • *Super Grandpa*

Books in English:
• *The Moon Was at a Fiesta* • *The Twenty-five Mixtec Cats*
• *Uncle Snake* • *Cool Melons – Turn to Frogs!* • *Ten Oni Drummers*

Books in Spanish:
• *Superabuelo (with audio CD)* • *Los veinticinco gatos mixtecos*
• *La Luna se fue de fiesta* • *Tío Culebra*

Table of Contents

More stuff at the back of the book!

A letter from the author

Congratulations to all those who parent! Whether we care for one child or many, raising kids involves constant decisions. Do we first clean up the spill or give the baby more cereal? Do we let our toddler "help" in the kitchen or keep her a safe distance from the stove? Do we shop for food and clothes for school, or first bring our teen to his practice or game? Given the countless choices we must make, parents deserve a medal of honor just for getting through the day!

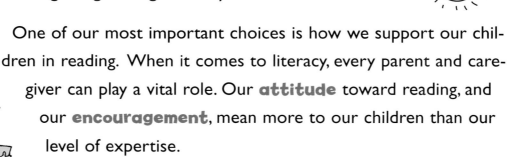

One of our most important choices is how we support our children in reading. When it comes to literacy, every parent and caregiver can play a vital role. Our **attitude** toward reading, and our **encouragement**, mean more to our children than our level of expertise.

When we raise kids to read, we give them a powerful gift. It is a gift that helps them succeed in school, stay out of trouble, and earn more money when they grow up. Since readers have access to more information, it's also a gift that can help children live longer, healthier lives.

Reading is the key to helping young people thrive! When young people read, they gain knowledge, vocabulary, insight, and perspective. That's why reading unlocks so many doors.

Imagine a society with less crime and violence, where people can more easily solve real problems. Imagine a society where every child can develop his or her unique abilities and skills. That's the kind of world we build when we raise young people to read.

The scope of this book is simple and to the point. It gives busy parents, grandparents, and other caregivers ideas to make children **want** to read. How can you prepare your baby for reading? What about getting teens to read in their spare time?

Raising a reader takes time and patience. But it's a thrilling journey packed with adventure that will bring your family closer together. Reading aloud to your child is an investment that will bear fruit long after the joyful memory fades. I hope the other reading "customs" in this book will also bring pleasure and lasting benefit to your child.

See which ideas work well for your family. Don't hold back. Give the gift! Your children and grandchildren will be glad you did.

With best wishes,

Matthew Gollub

A.M. Kindergarten

Did you know?

The best way for children to get ready for school is to hear at least 1,000 stories before kindergarten. Once children hear 1,000 stories, they have the knowledge, vocabulary, and attention span to follow all that their teacher is saying. They will also have an easier time making out printed words.

Word books, rhyming books, and a variety of picture books all count toward 1,000 stories. Even hearing the same book more than once counts toward a child's 1,000 stories.

Sharing 1,000 stories out loud with your child may seem like a lot, but you have 1,825 days together by the time your child turns 5.

P.M. Kindergarten

5 years x **365** days =
1825 reading days
before kindergarten starts!

There's no day like today to share a book out loud!

1. Read to your child every day.

HINT: Cuddle with your child while reading aloud. Giving your child your full attention is an excellent use of time!

HINT: Most elementary schools lack male teachers. Children need to see the MEN in their lives read, or they may grow up thinking that reading's just for girls!

HINT: Ask family members and caregivers to read to your child, too!

2. Show your child that reading is useful.

HINT:
Point out signs and explain new words as you take your child through the day.

HINT:
Talk about fine print in ways your child can understand.

HINT: Get caught in the act of reading.
Kids imitate what they observe.

HINT: Not reading can be a dangerous thing!

3. Show your child that reading is FUN.

HINT: Allow your children to move around and act out what they hear.

HINT: Talk to your child about what you're reading and let them know why it's interesting.

HINT: Kids love hearing how books relate to THEM — and to YOU!

HINT: TELLING stories and talking about the pictures in books is also great for kids.

4. Visit the library often—it's free!

HINT: Librarians want to help you! Introduce your child and ask for suggestions.

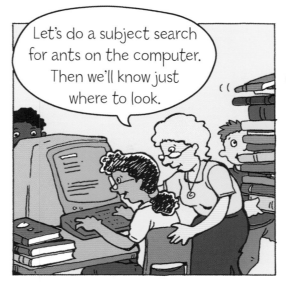

HINT: The two largest categories of books in a library are fiction (make-believe) and nonfiction (information).

HINT: To find out about free children's events at your library, just give them a call!

5. Keep plenty of books at home.

HINT: Children should have a variety of books within reach. Try storing books and magazines in bins under the bed.

Nathaniel is not in the mood for a storybook.

Today, the thought of insects makes his skin crawl.

Ah-hah. It was the joke book he was after!

HINT:
Some libraries let you RENEW books by phone or over the Internet.

HINT: Think of yourself as the household librarian. Which books should be on display this week?

6. Limit time spent on TV and video games.*
*Note: This is not a popular tip among kids.

HINT: The language in books is far richer than TV and necessary to do well in school.

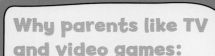

Why kids like TV and video games:
- lively content grabs attention
- little or no practice required
- no tests, no homework
- can share with friends
- available 24/7 at home

Why parents like TV and video games:
- doesn't seem to cost much
- keeps kids "safe" and busy
- no fuss, no mess
- gives parents free time
- can be enjoyed together

The problems with too much TV and video games:
- shortens children's attention span
- makes healthier activities seem boring
- can contribute to weight problems
- steals away precious hours from talking, interacting, homework, reading, and learning special skills

How to save kids from TOO MUCH electronic media

- Lovingly explain to them from an early age why too much "media" is not good.

- Be a model of moderation. If you watch loads of videos and TV, your kids will likely do the same.

- Give kids fun alternatives like sports, board games, arts and crafts, and media-less playtime with friends.

- Keep TVs and computers in central places so you're aware of how much (and what) your child is viewing.

- Before leaving older kids alone, help them plan how they'll use their time.

- **Be firm!** Withhold "media privileges" when homework, chores, and goals are not completed.

4:00 P.M.
Video Games OK

4:30 P.M.
No Video Games

HINT:
Decide on a TV and video game allowance. For example, try 30 minutes per day. Then let your child know when it's time to do something else.

7. Help your child read on the go.

HINT: Waiting time is READING time! Keep books ready in your car or purse.

HINT: When you don't have a book handy, read something else!

HINT: Keep an eye out for free written information.

HINT: Songs, stories, and recorded books also help prepare kids to read. Ask for audio books at your library.

8. Celebrate good reading effort.

HINT: Try keeping a reading log. Whether you or your child does the reading, every book counts.

HINT: Celebrate reading the way you celebrate sports.

HINT: Don't forget to celebrate YOUR reading efforts, too!

HINT: If all else fails, consider letting kids earn pocket change or privileges by reading in their spare time.

9. Be part of a reading community.

HINT: It's parent involvement that makes schools great!

HINT: When kids meet an author in person, it can change their relationship with books. Authors often speak at libraries and bookstores—maybe even at your child's school!

24

HINT: Bookstore staff can offer recommendations and help you find the right book for your child.

HINT: Consider starting a reading club outside of school with classmates and neighbors.

10. Use reading to connect with your teen.

HINT:
Keep an eye out for articles of interest to your teen.

HINT:
Tape useful reading material for your teen to the fridge, the mirror, or the bathroom floor—somewhere he or she is sure to look.

HINT: Set goals with your teen and work step by step toward the future.

HINT: Reading aloud with teens helps keep you in touch.

If you want to stay up a LITTLE longer, you can read a few extra minutes to yourself.

More hints for giving the gift

HINT: Place books (not a TV) in your child's room, and perhaps a reading lamp by your child's bed.

HINT: Writing is a natural complement to reading! Encourage your child to keep a journal. For starters, set an easy goal like just two sentences a day. Let kids choose their topic and express themselves!

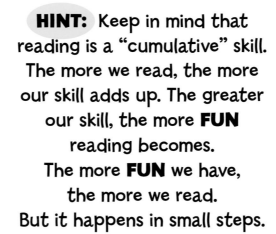

My Journal

$ENSE!

HINT: Have your older kids read to the younger ones. Older children can serve as role models and free up time for YOU!

HINT: Keep in mind that reading is a "cumulative" skill. The more we read, the more our skill adds up. The greater our skill, the more **FUN** reading becomes. The more **FUN** we have, the more we read. But it happens in small steps.

+ = **FUN**

HINT: Reading for PLEASURE can build needed confidence in preteens and teenagers. Consider BUYING books for your kids, but making them use their OWN money to buy things like video games.

Further reading

For heaps more suggestions about reading and recommended children's books, check out the following resources for grown-ups:

Books

The Read-Aloud Handbook by Jim Trelease
Reading Magic by Mem Fox
How to Get Your Child to Love Reading by Esmé Raji Codell
Walter and Valerie's Best Books for Children by Valerie Lewis and Walter Mayes
Read All About It by Jim Trelease*
*Contains inspired read-aloud selections for preteens and teens

Websites

www.acs.ucalgary.ca/~dkbrown A fine website for children's literature
www.ldonline.org For information about learning disabilities
www.csusm.edu/csb/ For recommended books in Spanish, or about Hispanic culture
www.infoplease.com Quick reference for general knowledge—very helpful for homework!

Facts to wrap your brain around

Did you know? Reading is not just "decoding" symbols on a page. It's a complicated process that draws on logic, sense of language, and background knowledge. That's why it's so helpful for kids to hear many stories before they attempt to read and write.

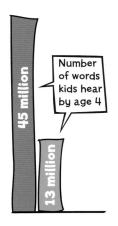

45 million

13 million

Number of words kids hear by age 4

Talk, talk, talk! Conversation stimulates a child's brain development. But the amount of conversation that kids hear varies by household. By age 4, some kids hear up to 45 million words total while others hear just 13 million.[1] The kids who hear more words have a huge advantage. The more times children hear words in conversation, the more easily they will make sense of the words in print. Stimulate your children from the time they are born with gentle questions and conversation. Give them verbal encouragement, and share your thoughts!

Vocabulary counts. How many different words do kids need to know? Most conversation between grown-ups and children involve a vocabulary of just 1,000 words.[2] Most daily conversation between adults uses a vocabulary of just 5,000 words.[3] But in school, kids will encounter 19,000 different words in printed text through the end of 4th grade![4] How will they learn all those extra words? The fastest and most fun way for kids to build their vocabulary is to read and be read to from books and magazines.

Out of school
91%

In school
9%

TV language is much simpler than print. The vocabulary used on television is from a lower grade level than nearly all forms of print media.[5] TV also uses much shorter sentences. On TV shows popular among teenagers, 72% of the sentences average just 7 words.[6] Even children's PICTURE books such as *Make Way for Ducklings* and *The Tales of Peter Rabbit* contain much longer sentences than TV and language that is at least twice as complex.[7]

10 hours a week, or 10 hours a day?

The 10-Hour Tipping Point. When children spend more than 10 hours per week on TV, DVDs and video games combined, their grades start to suffer. True, educational programs can inform and enrich. But generally, after this 10-hour tipping point, the more kids watch, the less they achieve in school.[8] Is TV the problem? The TV is a box. The problem is letting kids spend tons of time in front of it!

What's up with guys? In 1969, about 59% of students enrolled in college were men. By 1979, that number dropped to 49%. By 2004, just 43% of students enrolled in colleges in the U.S. were men.[9] At least 57% of college students are women! For decades, girls have done better than boys in elementary, middle and high school.[10] Could it be that boys who lack reading role models don't consider it "manly" to study hard?

Who has the best chance to influence kids? By the time they turn 6, kids will have spent 700 hours in school and about 52,000 hours OUTSIDE of school.[11] As the years go on, children spend 9% of their lives IN school and 91% OUTSIDE of school.[12] School teachers alone cannot ensure a child's success. Teachers need the support of parents, grandparents, aunts, uncles, and nannies who play a role in each child's life. It's these teachers OUTSIDE of school that influence kids most—and the parents especially who can instill the notion to read.

Reading gets us where we want to be!

1. Betty Hart and Todd Risley, "Meaningful Differences in the Everyday Experience of Young American Children" (Brookes Publishing, 1995) pp. 197-9. 2. Donald P. Hayes and Margaret G. Ahrens, "Vocabulary Simplification for Children: A Special Case for 'Motherese,'" *Journal of Child Language* vol. 15, 1988, pp. 395-410. 3. Ibid. 4. T.G. White, M.F. Graves, and W.H. Slater, "Growth of Reading Vocabulary in Divers Elementary Schools: Decoding and Word Meaning," *Journal of Educational Psychology* vol. 82, number 2, 1990, p. 286. 5. Jim Trelease, *The Read-Aloud Handbook* (Penguin Books, 2001) pp. 203-4. 6. Michael Lieberman, "The Verbal Language of Television," *The Journal of Reading*, April 1983, pp. 602-9. 7. Jim Trelease, *The Read-Aloud Handbook* (Penguin Books, 2001) pp. 203-4. 8. Patricia A. Williams, Edward H. Haertel, Geneva D. Haertel, and Herbert J. Walberg, "The Impact of Leisure-Time Television on School Learning: A Research Synthesis," *American Educational Research Journal*, Spring 1982, vol. 19, no. 1, pp. 19-50. 9. Thomas Mortenson, www.postsecondary.org/ti/ti_22.asp "The Weaker Sex...What's Still Wrong with the Guys?" Number 152, Feb. 2005. 10. National Center for Education Statistics, Digest of Education Statistics 2004, Table 110, "Average Student Scale Score in Reading by Age," 1971-2004. 11. Gerald W. Bracey, "Time Outside School," *Phi Delta Kappan*, September 1991, p. 88 "Starting at birth, a child spends only 9 percent of his or her life in school, 91 percent of it elsewhere." 12. Ibid.

Text copyright © 2007 by Matthew Gollub
Illustrations copyright © 2007 by Tortuga Press

Printed in China
Book design and illustration coloring by Karen Hanke
Print management by The Kids at Our House
2   3   4   5   6   7   8   9

Library of Congress Cataloging-in-Publication Data

Gollub, Matthew.
   Give the gift!: 10 fulfilling ways to raise a lifetime reader
   /by Matthew Gollub; illustrated by Larry Nolte.—1st ed.
   p. cm.
   Includes bibliographical references and index.
   ISBN-13: 978-1-889910-41-3 (hardcover: alk. paper)
   ISBN-13: 978-1-889910-42-0 (pbk.: alk. paper)
   1.Reading—Parent participation. 2.Parenting. 3.Parent and child.
   4.Children—Books and reading. I.Title.
   LB1050.2.G65 2007 649'.58—dc22
   2006015943

Portions of this book are also available in 8-page literacy booklets titled
5 Fun Tips to Raise a Lifetime Reader and
5 maneras de hacer que su niño lea para siempre. (Spanish edition)
To order bulk quantities of either this book or the shorter literacy booklets,
or to co-publish these items with your organization, please contact Tortuga Press.

TORTUGA PRESS
PMB: 181 2777 Yulupa Ave. Santa Rosa, CA 95405
Toll free: 1-866-4-TORTUGA www.tortugapress.com

Matthew Gollub

lives with his family in Santa Rosa, California. He enjoys reading in English, Spanish, and Japanese. An award-winning children's book author and dynamic storyteller, he speaks at schools and conferences around the U.S. He also plays drums and coaches kids' soccer. Ask for his books at your local library or bookstore, and visit him at **www.matthewgollub.com**

Larry Nolte

lives with his family in St. Louis, Missouri. His passion since grade school has been to doodle and draw. Because he is a reader, he has developed his talent into a career as a cartoonist and book illustrator. Please visit Larry at **www.larrynolte.com**